Business Plan Example

By
Kris Solie-Johnson

Published by
American Institute of Small Business
7515 Wayzata Blvd, Suite 129
Minneapolis, MN 55426
952-545-7001
www.aisb.biz
info@aisb.biz

Copyright 2003 American Institute of Small Business
ISBN 0-939069-73-3
Library of Congress

TABLE OF CONTENTS

INTRODUCTION

Going into business, either independently or with others, is a dream that most American would like to fulfill during their lifetime. Each year more than 1 million new businesses start up, while more than three to four times that number never leave the planning or thinking stage.

It has often been said that SMALL BUSINESSES come and go just like NIGHT and DAY. How often have you driven by a shopping center one week and observed a sign announcing a "GRAND OPENING"; then, within one year, driven by the same location, this time seeing a new sign saying: "GOING OUT OF BUSINESS SALE"?

How often do we hear stories about people and companies having a close or enter bankruptcy? And why is it that we keep hearing statistics that say: 9 out of 10 new businesses fail or close within the first two years of operations?

The answer can be found in any number of reasons. These reasons include:

- LOW SALES VOLUME
- INSUFFICIENT CAPITAL
- WRONG LOCATION
- INCORRECT MERCHANDISE
- COMPETITION IS TOO STRONG
- INEFFECTIVE ADVERTISING
- CHANGING MARKET CONDITIONS
- POOR MANAGEMENT
- LACK OF KNOW HOW

One could list a dozen more reasons why businesses fail. Regardless of the reason, the one way of **INSURING** a much higher degree of success when starting or opening a new business, expanding and diversifying an existing business or, even continuing with a current ongoing successful business is to have a **BUSINESS PLAN**.

WHY WRITE A BUSINESS PLAN?

There are many reasons why a business plan should be prepared. Regardless of the specific reason, the underlying goal of preparing a business plan is to insure the success of the business. In the end, a good business plan will give you a "GO" or "NO GO" answer for your business before you have invested all your time and money. Here are the other reasons why a business plan should be prepared:

1. To provide you with the ROAD MAP that you need in order to run your business. It allows you to make detours, change directions, and alter the pace that you set in starting and running the business.

2. To assist you in financing. Whether one is starting up a small business or buying a business, banks and financial institutions want to see that you know where you are, where you are going, and how you are going to get there.

3. To tell you how much money you need, when you will need it, and how you are going to get it and pay it back. In other words, how you will do your financing?

4. To help you clearly think through what type of business you are starting, and allows you to consider every aspect of that business.

5. To raise questions in a systematic way that you need to have the answered in order to succeed in your business.

6. To establish a system of checks and balances for your business so that you avoid mistakes.

7. To set up bench marks to keep your business under control.

8. To help you develop the COMPETITIVE SPIRIT to make you keenly prepared and ready to operate.

9. To make you think through the entire business process so that you do not open the business blindly or lack vital information in opening and maintaining your business.

10. To force you to analyze the competition.

AISB Quickie Business Plan

Page 1 **Introduction**

Company Name: _____

Date: _____

Your Name: _____

Your Idea/Concept: _____

Page 2 **Evaluating Ideas and Concepts**

Does the Test Market like our idea? _____

What did they like about it? _____

How many said they will buy it? _____

What price were they willing to pay? _____

Why would they buy ours vs. competition? _____

What need are we filling? _____

Page 3 **Researching Your Idea**

Industry opportunities/challenges: _____

Market size: _____

Competition strengths: _____

Site Location: _____

Business Formation: _____

Page 4 **Preliminary Planning**

Financial Plan

Start Up Costs: _____

Sales: Yr 1 _____   Yr 2 _____

Expenses: Yr 1 _____   Yr 2 _____

Profits: Yr 1 _____   Yr 2 _____

Marketing Plan

Product: _____

Price: _____

Promotion: _____

_____

Place: _____

Selling Plan: _____

Operation Plan

Units built: _____

Total Cost: _____

Unit Cost: _____

Page 5   **Getting Money**

Amount Needed: _____

Borrowed $: _____

Cash on Hand: _____

Cash for Equity of Company: _____ Equity given up: _____ %

Page 6   **Setting Up The Business**

People Needed: _____

Duties: _____

Technology Needed: _____

Advisors: _____   _____

_____   _____

Suppliers: _____   _____

_____   _____

BUSINESS PLAN OUTLINE

I. Cover Sheet and Table of Contents

II. Executive Summary

    A. Mission Statement

    B. Description of the Business

        1. Overall purpose of the business

        2. Specific purpose of the business

    C. Marketing Strategy

    D. Production Process

    E. Management Team

    F. Objectives of the Team

    G. Financial Considerations

        1. Income Statements (3 years)

        2. Balance Sheet Projections (3 years)

        3. Cash flow Projections (1 year)

III. Company Information

    A. Location(s)

        1. Location costs

        2. Location benefits

    B. Suppliers

IV. Industry, Market and Competition

    A. What is the Industry – Definition

        1. Background of industry

2. Trade Associations

3. Publications

4. Industry trends

5. Number and kinds of firms in the industry

6. Major influences

    a) Business cycle

    b) Natural resources

    c) Government Regulations

    d) Business Cycle

    e) Foreign influences

B. *Market Definition*

1. Customer Profile

2. Total market size

3. Market growth

C. *Competition*

V. Products and Services

A. *Initial Products and Services*

B. *Proprietary Features*

1. Patents

2. Copyrights

3. Unique or different features

C. *Future Products and Services*

1. New products and services

BUSINESS PLAN

THE MOUNTAIN SANDWICH SHOP

December 2003

By: Mary and George Johnson
1620 Hillsdale
Anywhere, Colorado

TABLE OF CONTENTS

EXECUTIVE SUMMARY

MISSION STATEMENT

The mission of THE MOUNTAIN SANDWICH SHOP is to serve high quality, healthy sandwiches and soups at moderate to high prices.

BUSINESS DESCRIPTION

THE MOUNTAIN SANDWICH SHOP will be a quick-service sandwich and soup restaurant. The food will be high quality and healthier than typical fast food places. The restaurant will offer take out and counter service with tables available for eating in the store. The restaurant will be located just west on U.S. Interstate 70, the 216 interchange exit in Anywhere, Colorado. It will be open seven days a week serving lunch and dinner. A breakfast menu will be added in three months after the opening. Prices will be moderate to high compared to the franchised sandwich shops.

MARKETING STRATEGY

The great majority of customers will come from Interstate 70 and surrounding businesses. Accordingly, heavy use of billboard advertising will be made to attract customers. Other media will include Ski Resort and Motel/Hotel advertising, and web site ordering.

PRODUCTION PROCESS

Many of the ingredients used in menu can be supplied locally. Even though management is assured of overnight deliveries, a 3-day inventory of all food items will be maintained in either a walk-in cooler or freezer to insure high quality of fresh ingredients.

MANAGEMENT TEAM

Mary and George Johnson will own 100% of the capital stock of the corporation. Each will own 50% of the outstanding stock. George Johnson is President. Mary Johnson is Vice President and Secretary.

OBJECTIVES OF THE TEAM

It is the objective of the team to operate the business with a minimal first year loss and have an operating profit by the first quarter of the second year of operations. The principals will pay themselves a minimum salary so as not to imperil the cash flow of the business.

FINANCIAL CONSIDERATION

Anticipated profits for the first years of operations are forecast as follows:

Year 1	$ 17,065
Year 2	$119,550
Year 3	$103,205

Sources of the necessary funds for financing the business are as follows:

Building Mortgage by First National Bank	$125,000
Working Capital by First National Bank	$75,000
Johnson Savings	$54,167
Total Sources of Funds	$254,167

INDUSTRY, MARKET AND COMPETITION

MARKET DEFINITION

CUSTOMER PROFILE

The primary market for THE MOUNTAIN SANDWICH SHOP is that of the Interstate 70 Highway travelers going in both east and west directions. These travelers are primarily vacationers and those driving long distances to and from ski resorts from Denver, Colorado. Their primary vehicle is the automobile.

It is expected that the minimum number of passengers per vehicle will be two. There will be some seasonality to the business in view of the much heavier traffic that is expected on the interstate during the winter months and late summer months.

TOTAL MARKET SIZE

Traffic count studies made by the Colorado Department of Transportation indicates the following average motor vehicle traffic flow in front of the restaurant location:

> Interstate 70   28,570 total vehicles daily
>
> 3,033 commercial trucks
>
> 25,537 cars

During the months of April, May, September and October the traffic counts are slightly lower than above for actual counts in 2002. This area of Interstate 70 is expected to have the following traffic counts in the years to come:

> 2004   30,670
>
> 2005   31,370
>
> 2006   32,070

4

2007	32,770

In addition to this very high traffic flow, Colorado State Highway 6 has some 6,000 vehicles and Colorado State Highway 40 has another 5,000 vehicles in average daily traffic flow.

Finally, within the counties of Summit and Eagle (west of restaurant), there are approximately 23,548 and 41,659 residents, respectfully. The populations of these counties is expected to grow to 28,140 and 48,667 in 2005 and 32,510 and 55,152 in 2010.

All of these traffic flow figures make for a very large potential market. Management strongly believes that 85% of their customer base will come from the Interstate. An additional 10% will come from Colorado State Highway 6 and Colorado State 40.

Only 5% of the total volume of business and customers are expected to come from the local population. Initially however, business from the local community will be somewhat higher simply because of curiosity.

MARKET GROWTH

According to the National Restaurant Association (NRA), the restaurant industry had its 11th consecutive year of real sales growth for 2002. In the latest NRA 2003 Restaurant Industry Forecast, a majority (57%) of quick-service restaurant operators expect business to get even better in 2003. The National Restaurant Association predicts that the sales for Limited Service Eating Places will increase 4.1% in 2003. Projected sales for all Limited Service Eating Places will be over $120.9 billion in 2003, compared to $116 billion in 2002.

At a state level, the Mountain Region of the United States is expected to lead the nation with eating-place-sales growth of 6.6%. This is being fueled by steady growth in employment,

5

population and disposable personal income. Colorado's sales are expected to grow from $5.9 million in 2002 to $6.3 million in 2003.

COMPETITION

The town of Anywhere has four eating establishments and one facility for lodging. With the exception of Mario's, all of the other eating establishments are located within Anywhere and away from the Interstate Highway 70 exit. They are not visible from the highway. A brief description of each is as follows:

T.J.'S BARBECUE: A barbecue house that serves both lunches and dinners with moderate pricing.

SMITH'S: Specializes in sandwiches, including hamburgers and hot dogs. Serves breakfast and is the oldest continuous operating restaurant in Anywhere.

HARDEE'S: Very successful food operation, and is the only fast food restaurant in Anywhere. It's very popular with both the highway tourist traffic and the local citizenry. It's open for breakfast and into the late hours of the evening.

MARIO'S: Busiest restaurant. It attracts customers from U.S. Interstate I-70 since it is the only truck stop in the area. It is quite popular and is visible from the Interstate.

HARDEE'S and MARIO'S are mentioned in national automobile publications. They also have billboard advertising, and HARDEE'S is able to take advantage of national advertising in view of its national affiliation. MARIO'S, a truck stop, is well known within trucking circles.

The fact that MARIO'S and HARDEE'S have such visibility is considered an advantage to THE MOUNTAIN SANDWICH SHOP, bringing traffic off the exit of I-70. It is anticipated that the restaurant will be able to capture part of their customer base.

It is anticipated that additional competition will come into the market as new fast food franchises develop. For example, some of the food operations starting up throughout the country include:

7

SUBWAY

STARBUCK'S COFFEE

THE SPAGHETTI FACTORY

STEWART'S ICE CREAM AND SANDWICHES

COMPETITION STRENGTHS AND WEAKNESSES

Competitive Strengths

1. HARDEE'S is a national franchise with a highly favorable reputation for both food quality and speed of service. In addition, it has both a very strong advertising campaign and high name recognition. It is especially popular with the children of many tourists, the primary drawing population by the restaurant.

2. MARIO'S has an excellent reputation. Its location puts the restaurant into a very competitive position with the restaurant since it is located off of the I-70 exit.

3. Both of the above competitors are open for breakfast.

4. Both of the above restaurants, as well as the two others in Anywhere, are popular with the local population.

5. SMITH'S is the oldest restaurant in the community. As a result it has a very large following with the local citizenry. It is a particularly popular breakfast especially with the local farming community having been in the area for two generations.

6. T.J.'S BARBECUE has a very strong local flavor in the decor and its furnishings. The menu is written on a chalk board and conveys a typical southern barbecue rib eating experience.

Competitive Weaknesses

1. None of the competitors will offer the freshness and quality of the menu which is offered by THE MOUNTAIN SANDWICH SHOP. The menu will be an attraction for many of

8

the I-70 Interstate drivers.

2. Only MARIO's is located adjacent to the exit, which means the restaurant will compete with only one other restaurant for its clientele.

3. SMITH'S has no advertising or visibility from the Interstate. In addition, it is located several blocks from the Interstate Exit.

4. T.J.'S BARBECUE has a very unattractive appearance from the outside which will leave potential customers with a questionable potential eating experience.

5. The mere name of the restaurant: THE MOUNTAIN SANDWICH SHOP will offer considerable curiosity appeal to some vehicle occupants, thus bringing in a certain amount of traffic.

6. THE MOUNTAIN SANDWICH SHOP anticipates being open evenings until 10:00 PM, thus enabling it to capture late evening Interstate Traffic heading back to Denver as well as from the local community.

PRODUCTS AND SERVICES

INITIAL PRODUCTS

Homemade Soups

Served Daily:
    Chicken Noodle
    Creamy Tomato
    Beefy Vegetable

Daily Specials:

Split Pea	Cheese and Broccoli Soup	Black Bean Soup
Chicken Vegetable	Squash Potato Chowder	Tortellini Soup
Clam Chowder	Tortilla Soup	Tuscan Chicken Soup

Sandwiches

Customers can choose from the following list to create their own sandwich:

Meats	Cheeses	Bread	Vegies	Condiments
Roast Beef	Swiss	White	Lettuce	Mayo
Corn Beef	Cheddar	Wheat	Cucumber	Butter
Ham	Pepper Jack	Bagel	Tomato	Mustard
Salami	Mozzarella	Baguette	Bean Sprouts	Dijon Mustard
Turkey	Colby	Asigo Cheese	Avocado	Oil & Vinegar
Smoked Turkey	Provolone	Croissant	Green Pepper	Ketchup
Pastrami	American	Rye	Onion	Horseradish
Humus	Co-Jack	Pumpernickel	Jalapenos	Margarine

Sides and Desserts

Various Chips	Cut Vegetables	Fruit cups
Energy Bars	Candy Bars	Large Homemade Cookies

Beverages

Coffee	Hot Teas	Milk
Coca Cola Products	Flavored Juices	Hot Chocolate (different flavors)
Chai	Bottled Water	

Miscellaneous Take-Out Items

Packaged Mustards	Milk and Cream	Butter
Cream Cheese	Assorted Cheeses	

Paper Napkins, Plates   Plastic Dinnerware

UNIQUE FEATURES OF THE MENU

The entire menu has been patterned after successful sandwich shops in Minneapolis, Minnesota. Most of the items are unavailable at the level of freshness and quality at other Anywhere restaurants.

The menu itself will have a number of featured items. Each of these items will have a name together with an identifiable Mountain Range. Some of the named items will include:

> Pike's Peak Corned Beef
> The Everest Vegy Melt
> The K2 Turkey Club
> The McKinley Roast Beef
> The Ranier Humus Express

Because of the menu and the marketing strategy, management forecasts approximately 80 to 85% of its business will come from the Interstate I-70. Approximately 10 to 15% of its business will come from Colorado State Highway 6 and Colorado State Highway 40. Only 5% of the restaurants business is expected to come from the local community. However, over a period of time, it is expected that **THE MOUNTAIN SANDWICH SHOP** will become a popular eating and gathering place for local residents. Thus, the business with local residents will eventually account for 10% of the total volume of business.

The business with local residents will even have greater impetus when the Johnson's begin offering their breakfast menu.

All items on the menu will be available for TAKE-OUT.

FUTURE BREAKFAST MENU

The final menu has not yet been determined but will include such items as: Eggs, Pancakes, Hash Brown Potatoes, Bacon Ham, English Muffins, Sausage, Toast, Danish Pastries, Bagels, Muffins, Fruit Juices, Fresh Fruit in Season, and Oatmeal. It is expected to begin serving breakfasts approximately three months after the initial opening of THE MOUNTAIN SANDWICH SHOP.

MARKETING PLAN

OVERVIEW

THE MOUNTAIN SANDWICH SHOP will offer high quality food at moderate prices compared to the pricing of typical franchise sandwich shops. However, the menu prices for THE MOUNTIAN SANDWICH SHOP will be slightly higher than the comparable sandwiches at other Anywhere franchised food establishments.

Quick service will be available at the counter and tables are available for eating. Take-out service will also be available. The owners recognize that Interstate 70 is the main highway traveled by tourists coming from Denver and going to a large number of ski resorts.

Sandwich and soups are immensely popular with these tourists when heading to a ski hill. Thus, a restaurant such as THE MOUNTAIN SANDWICH SHOP will be a welcome change and relief to these tourists from the conventional franchised fast food establishments that they normally find along an interstate highway.

THE MOUNTAIN SANDWICH SHOP will be open for business seven days a week. Initially it will provide luncheon and dinner service to its patrons, remaining open until the early hours of the evening. Both cold and hot dish selections, together with unique desserts, will be available.

Mary and George Johnson believe that a very viable business opportunity exists for the opening of a sandwich shop at the exit of U.S. Interstate 70 in Anywhere. In view of the proposed location of the delicatessen, the anticipated restaurant business should be excellent.

MARKETING OBJECTIVES

The primary objective of THE MOUNTAIN SANDWICH SHOP will be to attract customers from the very heavily traveled U.S. Interstate 70 Highway. These customers are mostly tourists traveling between the Denver and the heavily visited ski resort areas. Additional customers will come from local businesses around the ski areas.

A second marketing objective will be to gain repeat customers from those who patronize the restaurant for the first time as well as to gain customers through word of mouth advertising from first time users. This will be done by serving high quality food in pleasant surroundings and a clean comfortable atmosphere. In addition, the take out food will be insulated to stay warm or cold while the customer is skiing.

MARKETING STRATEGY-ADVERTISING AND PROMOTION

An important consideration in the total marketing effort of the restaurant is found in the quality of the food and the convenience in taking it to the ski resorts. This theme of high quality and easy to take to the ski hills will be a main part of the marketing campaign.

Since it is anticipated that the great majority of customers who will patronize THE MOUNTAIN SANDWICH SHOP will be tourists using U.S. Interstate 70, the restaurant will make wide use of billboard advertising. An important feature of the building purchase and land lease includes the use of four large billboards, two on each side of I-70 approximately one and one half miles from the Anywhere exit going in both east and west directions, and two similar signs located approximately 5 miles from the Anywhere exit in the same manner. The use of these billboards is for the remaining three years of the current land lease, and subject to renegotiation at that time.

Additional billboard locations will be placed on both Colorado State 6 and Colorado State 40

13

highways. It is expected that the billboards will carry the same message and theme of the quality and convenience of the meals.

Since the name THE MOUNTAIN SANDWICH SHOP menu will have a mountain theme, the use of famous mountain names will be used. This will be particularly employed for the interior setting and design of the facility in addition to some menu items. The format and decor of the restaurant will include log seats and tables, a fireplace, biographies of great mountain climbers and antique ski and climbing gear. With regards to the exterior of the building, the restaurant's name will be highlighted by two large spotlights in the evening hours.

At the take-out counter, the menu items will be displayed with antique camping kettles and flatware. The menus will have biographies of famous hikers and histories of mountain ranges. In addition, each menu item will contain names having a mountaineering theme. For example, "The Pike's Peak Reuben", "The Everest Vegy Melt", "The K2 Turkey Club", and so on. A likewise similar art and copy approach will be given to the point-of-purchase displays used throughout the restaurant. Items with a mountaineering theme will be used to give the interior a proper finishing touch. These will include pictures of famous hikers, history of mountain ranges, mountaineering and camping antiques and other rustic fixtures.

Restaurant items will be attractively displayed in refrigerated cases. Also, each of the dessert specialties will be similarly displayed in a refrigerated bakery display case. Such displays will give a high point-of-purchase advertising appeal to patrons.

In addition, all of the staff will wear camp shirts specially silk-screened with THE MOUNTAIN SANDWICH SHOP name and logo.

Finally, THE MOUNTAIN SANDWICH SHOP will operate a web site for people to e-mail or fax take-out orders before they leave their homes or hotels in Denver. Additional advertising will be in the hotels around Denver to help encourage business.

SALES

All sales will be for cash or major credit card. Credit cards from VISA, MASTER CARD, AMERICAN EXPRESS, and DISCOVER will be accepted. Checks will not be accepted.

THE PRODUCTION PLAN

FACILITY REQUIREMENTS

The restaurant will be located in a building immediately adjacent to the I-70 exit. This facility was a former restaurant. It has current seating of 60 and can be expanded to accommodate 90 persons at a very moderate cost.

Since it is a former restaurant, it contains very important restaurant equipment and fixtures which would be available for purchase together with the restaurant building. The asking price on the building is $130,000.

EQUIPMENT REQUIREMENTS

Equipment furnished with the building at a cost of $10,000 includes:

1-small desk	1-60 gal. water heater
1-2 compartment sink	1-6 X 10 walk-in cooler
2-6 X 8 walk-in freezer	1-small bake table
1-small bake oven	12-42 inch tables
44-black upholstery chairs	1-48 inch grill
2-19 quart deep fryers	1-pan steam unit
2-19 Hobart dishwasher	1-2 burner electric cooker
2-Sandwich Refrigerators	48-feet metal shelving

2-three ton heating and air conditioning units

1-6ft. stainless steel table

1-pint stainless steel up-draft unit with exhaust fan

Additional tableware, kitchen tools, and accessories will have to be purchased as well as the

following:

2-Microwave ovens   1-large refrigerator

1-cash register   1-scale

1-meat slicer   1-bread slicer

1-bakery display case   1-large freezer

1-refrigerated deli display case

LABOR REQUIREMENTS

The two principal positions needed to operate the deli are that of the Manager and the Cook. Both Mary and George Johnson will co-share these responsibilities. Arrangements have been made to take a special one week delicatessen cooking and food preparation course in Minneapolis, Minnesota.

The following employees and their projected monthly salaries are as follows:

Manager-Cook	George Johnson	$2,500
Co-Manager	Mary Johnson	2,500
Part-Time Cook		1,500
Waiters/Waitresses		2,400
Dishwasher/Custodial		1,300
Miscellaneous		1,500
TOTAL LABOR		**$11,700**

FOOD PREPARATION PROCESS

As a restaurant, many of the ingredients and final menu items will have to be supplied by local food and restaurant wholesalers. Freshness and quality are key to the success of this business.

17

Arrangements are being made to keep a one week minimum inventory of some items on hand at all times. This will be done with the use of the freezer and walk-in cooler. Arrangements have been made with the following food suppliers and wholesalers to provide for their specialty food requirements.

Each of these wholesalers has assured the Johnson's that they can deliver orders within 48 hours and, if necessary, deliver within 24 hours subject to an added delivery charge.

Fancy Foods, Boulder, CO.

Basic cooking ingredients like flour, sugar, and spices

National Food Products Company, Denver, Colorado

Meat and Cheese Products

Fruits, Roots and Herbs, Denver, Colorado

Fresh Vegetables and Fruits

Paper Planet, Denver, Colorado

Paper and container products

Hauser Foods, Denver, Colorado

A back-up supplier and wholesaler for all of the above products

Some purchases will be made on a periodic basis from Hauser Foods to assure the company of a second source of supply. All other food products and ingredients can be purchased from local wholesalers who make daily runs to Anywhere from neighboring Colorado cities. These include dairy products, fruits, vegetables, seasonings, baking needs, breads, canned goods, etc.

Deli meats will be stored in the refrigerated case until needed. All meats will be freshly sliced upon demand. Soups and breads will be prepared daily. Most desserts will be kept in the freezer until the day of use.

MANAGEMENT TEAM AND KEY PERSONNEL

Mary and George Johnson have incorporated their restaurant under the name of THE MOUNTAIN SANDWICH SHOP. George is the president while Mary is vice president and secretary. Each has 50% of the capital stock of the corporation.

With regards to the day-to-day operations, they have assumed the following titles:

Manager	George Johnson
Co-Manager	Mary Johnson

George expects to work 60 hours a week until the operation can afford additional staffing. Mary expects to work a 40 hour week. A number of part time employees will be hired. It is anticipated that a shift leader will be appointed. This leader will be trained to both open and close the restaurant in the absence of George and Mary Johnson.

The company's attorneys, Solie, Johnson and Hill Ltd. together with their Certified Public Accounting Firm of Holland and Webber have recommended that THE MOUNTAIN SANDWICH SHOP be set up as an S-Corp for Internal Revenue reporting purposes.

The business has been incorporated under the laws of the State of Colorado with the effective date being January 5, 2003.

BUSINESS ADVISORS

The following business advisors have been or will be used as needed:

Accountant: Judy Holland with Holland and Webber, Certified Public Accountants, Anywhere, CO

Lawyer:	Karen Solie with Solie, Johnson and Hill Ltd., Denver, CO
Banker:	Adam Johnston, President of Anywhere State Bank, Anywhere, CO
Insurance:	Emily Marshall with Marshall Insurance, Anywhere, CO
Advertising:	Marsha Forester of Forester and Forester Advertising Agency, Boulder, CO

THE FINANCIAL PLAN

SUMMARY

Taking into consideration that THE MOUNTAIN SANDWICH SHOP will be a new eating establishment catering to the highway traffic on U.S. Interstate 70, conservative accounting procedures and projections have been made. The following Income Projections are as follows for the first three years of operations for the restaurant:

	Profit/Loss
YEAR 1-	$ 17,065
YEAR 2-	$119,550
YEAR 3-	$103,205

Income Statement projections indicate that the restaurant will have a positive cash flow beginning with the eleventh month of operations. At that time it is forecast that monthly cash receipts will amount to $52,200 with expenses of $44,150. Until that time, the commercial loan from the Anywhere State Bank and the Johnson's investment should be sufficient to provide the restaurant with its necessary cash needs.

The three year balance sheet projects indicate that the net worth (Owner's Equity) of THE MOUNTAIN SANDWICH SHOP will be as follows:

YEAR 1- $18,065

YEAR 2- $120,550

YEAR 3-$104,205

The three year projections for INCOME STATEMENTS, CASH FLOW and BALANCE SHEETS are shown on the following pages.

Each of these spreadsheets has been prepared by the firm of Holland and Webber, Certified Public Accountants located in Anywhere, N.C. All of the cost information is supported by documented:

* Vendor and Supplier Cost Proposals

* Contractor Bids

* Local Wage and Salary Schedules

* Public Utility Estimates

* Letters of Financial Commitments

* Forester and Forester Advertising Proposal

* Bear and Marshall Insurance Estimate

SOURCES OF FUNDS

Building Mortgage 20 years at 10%	$160,000
Anywhere State Bank	
Commercial Loan, Anywhere State Bank	$75,000
7 years at 9%	
Cash from the Johnson's Savings and sale of some of their common stock	$54,167
Total Start-Up Funds	$289,167

The Anywhere State Bank has also agreed to provide THE MOUNTAIN SANDWICH SHOP with a line of credit amounting to $20,000 should it be necessary.

A recent appraisal by the firm of Smith, Blaisdel and Corona, commercial real estate appraisers of Denver, CO., of the proposed building which will be purchased by the Johnson's estimates the true value of the property to be worth $200,000. In view of the fact that it has been

unoccupied and that the estate of the former owners wishes to sell the property is the reason for the excellent purchase opportunity.

APPENDIX A

BIOGRAPHIES OF THE PRINCIPALS

George and Mary have been married for 18 years and have two children, Adam, age 16 and Emily, age 14. Mary Johnson has a degree from the University of North Carolina where she majored in elementary education. She taught for three years with the Brooklyn New York Department of Education. Upon moving to Anywhere, she has been teaching at the John Hay Elementary School in Anywhere. George is 42 years old and Mary is 40. They have lived in Anywhere for the past 15 years and participate in a number of community, school and church activities.

George Johnson received his degree in Textile Engineering and after spending three years as a Reserve Naval Officer took a position with the Yorkville Yarn Company in Anywhere. He has been with the company 15 years. His last position was Assistant Chief Engineer.

George has had considerable retail store experience since he worked at his father's hardware store while in high school and during his summer vacations while attending the University of Minnesota. During his term of service in the Navy, he was stationed at the Brooklyn Naval Shipyard and became very acquainted with restaurant operations.

This acquaintance gradually grew into a favorite pastime in that both expressed a desire to some day have their own restaurant business. They enjoyed the one-on-one interaction with both customers and employees.

Due to the fact that the Yorkville Yarn Company has been sold, and the company will be moved from Anywhere, George has been given the option of moving or losing his position. He and

Mary decided it would be in their best interest to start their own business. Accordingly, with their love of mountaineering and comfort food, they now wish to open their own restaurant. Mary has given notice that she will only be available for substitute teaching since both will devote full time to operating and running THE MOUNTAIN SANDWICH SHOP.

Year 1 Income Statement Projections for THE MOUNTAIN SANDWICH SHOP

		January	February	March	April	May	June	July	August	Sept	Oct	Nov	Dec	Totals
Number of Days in Month		31	28	31	30	31	30	31	31	30	31	30	31	
Number of Customers	Price													
Avg number of breakfast customers	$ 6					10	25	40	35	30	30	35	40	245
Avg number of lunch customers	$ 8	25	35	50	40	40	70	90	85	80	80	85	100	780
Avg number of dinner customers	$ 10	25	35	50	40	40	70	90	85	80	80	85	100	780
Revenues														
Breakfast check amt/Customer		$ -	$ -	$ -	$ -	$ 1,860	$ 4,500	$ 7,440	$ 6,510	$ 5,400	$ 5,580	$ 6,300	$ 7,440	
Lunch check amt/Customer		6,200	7,840	12,400	9,600	9,920	16,800	22,320	21,080	19,200	19,840	20,400	24,800	
Dinner check amt/Customer		7,750	9,800	15,500	12,000	12,400	21,000	27,900	26,350	24,000	24,800	25,500	31,000	
Total Revenues		$ 13,950	$ 17,640	$ 27,900	$ 21,600	$ 24,180	$ 42,300	$ 57,660	$ 53,940	$ 48,600	$ 50,220	$ 52,200	$ 63,240	$ 473,430
Cost of Goods	Cost													
Breakfast Cost of Goods	$ 3	$ -	$ -	$ -	$ -	$ 930	$ 2,250	$ 3,720	$ 3,255	$ 2,700	$ 2,790	$ 3,150	$ 3,720	
Lunch Cost of Goods	$ 4	3,100	3,920	6,200	4,800	4,960	8,400	11,160	10,540	9,600	9,920	10,200	12,400	
Dinner Cost of Goods	$ 5	3,875	4,900	7,750	6,000	6,200	10,500	13,950	13,175	12,000	12,400	12,750	15,500	
Total COGS		$ 6,975	$ 8,820	$ 13,950	$ 10,800	$ 12,090	$ 21,150	$ 28,830	$ 26,970	$ 24,300	$ 25,110	$ 26,100	$ 31,620	$ 236,715
Expenses														
Fixed Expenses														
Insurance		$ 500			$ 250			$ 250			$ 250			$ 1,250
Rent		1,000	1,000	1,000	1,000	1,000	1,000	1,000	1,000	1,000	1,000	1,000	1,000	12,000
Taxes & Licenses		500	500	500	500	500	500	500	500	500	500	500	500	6,000
Interest - Loan		500	500	500	500	500	500	500	500	500	500	500	500	6,000
Interest - Mortgage		1,300	1,300	1,300	1,300	1,300	1,300	1,300	1,300	1,300	1,300	1,300	1,300	15,600
Variable Expenses														
Salaries		$ 11,700	$ 11,700	$ 11,700	$ 11,700	$ 11,700	$ 11,700	$ 11,700	$ 11,700	$ 11,700	$ 11,700	$ 11,700	$ 11,700	140,400
Advertising		1,000	750	500	500	500	750	500	500	500	750	500	500	7,250
Dues & Subscriptions		100												100
Legal & Accounting		500	50	50	50	50	50	50	50	50	50	50	50	1,050
Office Supplies		150	150	150	150	150	150	150	150	150	150	150	150	1,800
Telephone		50	50	50	50	50	50	50	50	50	50	50	50	600
Utilities		800	800	800	800	800	800	800	800	800	800	800	800	9,600
Miscellaneous		1,500	1,500	1,500	1,500	1,500	1,500	1,500	1,500	1,500	1,500	1,500	1,500	18,000
Total Expenses		$ 19,600	$ 18,300	$ 18,050	$ 18,300	$ 18,050	$ 18,300	$ 18,300	$ 18,050	$ 18,050	$ 18,550	$ 18,050	$ 18,050	$ 219,650
Net Profit		$ (12,625)	$ (9,480)	$ (4,100)	$ (7,500)	$ (5,960)	$ 2,850	$ 10,530	$ 8,920	$ 6,250	$ 6,560	$ 8,050	$ 13,570	$ 17,065
Cumulative Profit		$ (12,625)	$ (22,105)	$ (26,205)	$ (33,705)	$ (39,665)	$ (36,815)	$ (26,285)	$ (17,365)	$ (11,115)	$ (4,555)	$ 3,495	$ 17,065	4%

Year 2 Income Statement Projections for THE MOUNTAIN SANDWICH SHOP

	Price/Cost	January	February	March	April	May	June	July	August	Sept	Oct	Nov	Dec	Totals
Number of Days in Month		31	28	31	30	31	30	31	31	30	31	30	31	
Number of Customers														
Avg number of breakfast customers		40	40	60	30	30	50	60	50	30	30	35	60	345
Avg number of lunch customers		100	100	120	90	90	110	120	110	90	90	95	120	1,235
Avg number of dinner customers		100	100	120	90	90	110	120	110	90	90	95	120	1,235
Revenues	Price													
Breakfast check amt/Customer	$6	7,440	6,720	11,160	5,400	5,580	9,000	11,160	9,300	5,400	5,580	6,300	11,160	
Lunch check amt/Customer	$8	24,800	22,400	29,760	21,600	22,320	26,400	29,760	27,280	21,600	22,320	22,800	29,760	
Dinner check amt/Customer	$10	31,000	28,000	37,200	27,000	27,900	33,000	37,200	34,100	27,000	27,900	28,500	37,200	
Total Revenues		$63,240	$57,120	$78,120	$54,000	$55,800	$68,400	$78,120	$70,680	$54,000	$55,800	$57,600	$78,120	$771,000
Cost of Goods	Cost													
Breakfast Cost of Goods	$3	3,720	3,360	5,580	2,700	2,790	4,500	5,580	4,650	2,700	2,790	3,150	5,580	
Lunch Cost of Goods	$4	12,400	11,200	14,880	10,800	11,160	13,200	14,880	13,640	10,800	11,160	11,400	14,880	
Dinner Cost of Goods	$5	15,500	14,000	18,600	13,500	13,950	16,500	18,600	17,050	13,500	13,950	14,250	18,600	
Total COGS		$31,620	$28,560	$39,060	$27,000	$27,900	$34,200	$39,060	$35,340	$27,000	$27,900	$28,800	$39,060	$385,500
Expenses														
Fixed Expenses														
Insurance		500			250			250			250			1,250
Rent		1,100	1,100	1,100	1,100	1,100	1,100	1,100	1,100	1,100	1,100	1,100	1,100	13,200
Taxes & Licenses		500	500	500	500	500	500	500	500	500	500	500	500	6,000
Interest - Loan		500	500	500	500	500	500	500	500	500	500	500	500	6,000
Interest - Mortgage		1,300	1,300	1,300	1,300	1,300	1,300	1,300	1,300	1,300	1,300	1,300	1,300	15,600
Variable Expenses														$-
Salaries		15,000	15,000	15,000	15,000	15,000	15,000	15,000	15,000	15,000	15,000	15,000	15,000	180,000
Advertising		500	750	500	500	500	750	500	500	500	750	500	500	6,750
Dues & Subscriptions		100												100
Legal & Accounting		500	50	50	50	50	50	50	50	50	50	50	50	1,050
Office Supplies		150	150	150	150	150	150	150	150	150	150	150	150	1,800
Telephone		50	50	50	50	50	50	50	50	50	50	50	50	600
Utilities		800	800	800	800	800	800	800	800	800	800	800	800	9,600
Miscellaneous		2,000	2,000	2,000	2,000	2,000	2,000	2,000	2,000	2,000	2,000	2,000	2,000	24,000
Total Expenses		$23,000	$22,200	$21,950	$22,200	$21,950	$22,200	$22,200	$21,950	$21,950	$22,450	$21,950	$21,950	$265,950
Net Profit		$8,620	$6,360	$17,110	$4,800	$5,950	$12,000	$16,860	$13,390	$5,050	$5,450	$6,850	$17,110	$119,550
Cumulative Profit		$8,620	$14,980	$32,090	$36,890	$42,840	$54,840	$71,700	$85,090	$90,140	$95,590	$102,440	$119,550	16%

Year 3 Income Statement Projections for THE MOUNTAIN SANDWICH SHOP

	Price/Cost	January	February	March	April	May	June	July	August	Sept	Oct	Nov	Dec	Totals
Number of Days in Month		31	28	31	30	31	30	31	31	30	31	30	31	
Number of Customers														
Avg number of breakfast customers		45	45	70	30	30	50	70	60	30	30	35	70	375
Avg number of lunch customers		110	110	130	90	90	110	130	120	90	90	95	130	1,295
Avg number of dinner customers		110	110	130	90	90	110	130	120	90	90	95	130	1,295
Revenues														
Breakfast check amt/Customer	$ 6	8,370	7,560	13,020	5,400	5,580	9,000	13,020	11,160	5,400	5,580	6,300	13,020	
Lunch check amt/Customer	$ 8	27,280	24,640	32,240	21,600	22,320	26,400	32,240	29,760	21,600	22,320	22,800	32,240	
Dinner check amt/Customer	$ 10	34,100	30,800	40,300	27,000	27,900	33,000	40,300	37,200	27,000	27,900	28,500	40,300	
Total Revenues		$ 69,750	$ 63,000	$ 85,560	$ 54,000	$ 55,800	$ 68,400	$ 85,560	$ 78,120	$ 54,000	$ 55,800	$ 57,600	$ 85,560	$ 813,150
Cost of Goods														
Breakfast Cost of Goods	$ 3	4,185	3,780	6,510	2,700	2,790	4,500	6,510	5,580	2,700	2,790	3,150	6,510	
Lunch Cost of Goods	$ 4	13,640	12,320	16,120	10,800	11,160	13,200	16,120	14,880	10,800	11,160	11,400	16,120	
Dinner Cost of Goods	$ 5	17,050	15,400	20,150	13,500	13,950	16,500	20,150	18,600	13,500	13,950	14,250	20,150	
Total COGS		$ 34,875	$ 31,500	$ 42,780	$ 27,000	$ 27,900	$ 34,200	$ 42,780	$ 39,060	$ 27,000	$ 27,900	$ 28,800	$ 42,780	$ 406,575
Expenses														
Fixed Expenses														
Insurance		$ 500			$ 250			$ 250			$ 250			$ 1,250
Rent		1,200	1,200	1,200	1,200	1,200	1,200	1,200	1,200	1,200	1,200	1,200	1,200	14,400
Taxes & Licenses		500	500	500	500	500	500	500	500	500	500	500	500	6,000
Interest - Loan		500	500	500	500	500	500	500	500	500	500	500	500	6,000
Interest - Mortgage		1,300	1,300	1,300	1,300	1,300	1,300	1,300	1,300	1,300	1,300	1,300	1,300	15,600
Variable Expenses													$ -	$ -
Salaries		17,000	17,000	17,000	17,000	17,000	17,000	17,000	17,000	17,000	17,000	17,000	17,000	204,000
Advertising		500	750	500	500	500	750	500	500	500	750	500	500	6,750
Dues & Subscriptions		200												200
Legal & Accounting		500	50	50	50	50	50	50	50	50	50	50	50	1,050
Office Supplies		150	150	150	150	150	150	150	150	150	150	150	150	1,800
Telephone		60	60	60	60	60	60	60	60	60	60	60	60	720
Utilities		800	800	800	800	800	800	800	800	800	800	800	800	9,600
Miscellaneous		3,000	3,000	3,000	3,000	3,000	3,000	3,000	3,000	3,000	3,000	3,000	3,000	36,000
Total Expenses		$ 26,210	$ 25,310	$ 25,060	$ 25,310	$ 25,060	$ 25,310	$ 25,310	$ 25,060	$ 25,060	$ 25,560	$ 25,060	$ 25,060	$ 303,370
Net Profit		$ 8,665	$ 6,190	$ 17,720	$ 1,690	$ 2,840	$ 8,890	$ 17,470	$ 14,000	$ 1,940	$ 2,340	$ 3,740	$ 17,720	$ 103,205
Cumulative Profit		$ 8,665	$ 14,855	$ 32,575	$ 34,265	$ 37,105	$ 45,995	$ 63,465	$ 77,465	$ 79,405	$ 81,745	$ 85,485	$ 103,205	13%

THE MOUNTAIN SANDWICH SHOP

Pro-Forma Balance Sheet

Start-Up

ASSETS

Cash	$	104,167
Inventories	$	-
Property	$	200,000
Equipment	$	10,000
Total Assets	**$**	**314,167**

LIABILITIES AND OWNER'S EQUITY

Account Payables	$	-
Anywhere Bank Loan	$	75,000
Anywhere Mortgage	$	160,000
Loan from Shareholders	$	54,167
Total Liabilities	**$**	**289,167**
Retained Earnings	$	24,000
Common Stock	$	1,000
Total Owner's Equity	**$**	**25,000**
Total Liabilities and Owner's Equity	**$**	**314,167**

THE MOUNTAIN SANDWICH SHOP

Pro-Forma Balance Sheet

End of Year 1

ASSETS

Cash	$	78,867
Inventories	$	63,124
Property	$	200,000
Equipment	$	12,000
Total Assets	**$**	**353,991**

LIABILITIES AND OWNER'S EQUITY

Account Payables	$	56,559
Anywhere Bank Loan	$	67,600
Anywhere Mortgage	$	157,600
Loan from Shareholders	$	54,167
Total Liabilities	**$**	**335,926**
Retained Earnings	$	17,065
Common Stock	$	1,000
Total Owner's Equity	**$**	**18,065**
Total Liabilities and Owner's Equity	**$**	**353,991**

THE MOUNTAIN SANDWICH SHOP

Pro-Forma Balance Sheet

End of Year 2

ASSETS

Cash	$	123,153
Inventories	$	77,649
Property	$	210,000
Equipment	$	23,242
Total Assets	**$**	**434,044**

LIABILITIES AND OWNER'S EQUITY

Account Payables	$	51,798
Anywhere Bank Loan	$	58,129
Anywhere Mortgage	$	154,400
Loan from Shareholders	$	49,167
Total Liabilities	**$**	**313,494**
Retained Earnings	$	119,550
Common Stock	$	1,000
Total Owner's Equity	**$**	**120,550**
Total Liabilities and Owner's Equity	**$**	**434,044**

THE MOUNTAIN SANDWICH SHOP

Pro-Forma Balance Sheet

End of Year 3

ASSETS

Cash	$	106,388
Inventories	$	83,514
Property	$	210,000
Equipment	$	25,612
Total Assets	**$**	**425,514**

LIABILITIES AND OWNER'S EQUITY

Account Payables	$	77,442
Anywhere Bank Loan	$	48,500
Anywhere Mortgage	$	151,200
Loan from Shareholders	$	44,167
Total Liabilities	**$**	**321,309**
Retained Earnings	$	103,205
Common Stock	$	1,000
Total Owner's Equity	**$**	**104,205**
Total Liabilities and Owner's Equity	**$**	**425,514**

Year 1 Cash Flow Projections for THE MOUNTAIN SANDWICH SHOP

	Pre Start-Up	January	February	March	April	May	June	July	August	Sept	Oct	Nov	Dec
Beginning Cash	$ -	$ 234,417	$ 221,343	$ 210,913	$ 205,864	$ 197,415	$ 190,507	$ 192,409	$ 201,991	$ 209,963	$ 215,265	$ 220,877	$ 227,978
Sales	$ -	$ 13,950	$ 17,640	$ 27,900	$ 21,600	$ 24,180	$ 42,300	$ 57,660	$ 53,940	$ 48,600	$ 50,220	$ 52,200	$ 63,240
Bank Loan	75,000												
Bank Loan Mortgage	160,000												
Shareholder's Loan	54,167												
Total Receipts	$ 289,167	$ 13,950	$ 17,640	$ 27,900	$ 21,600	$ 24,180	$ 42,300	$ 57,660	$ 53,940	$ 48,600	$ 50,220	$ 52,200	$ 63,240
Purchases	$ 25,000	$ 6,975	$ 8,820	$ 13,950	$ 10,800	$ 12,090	$ 21,150	$ 28,830	$ 26,970	$ 24,300	$ 25,110	$ 26,100	$ 31,620
Insurance	500				250			250			250		
Rent	2,000	1,000	1,000	1,000	1,000	1,000	1,000	1,000	1,000	1,000	1,000	1,000	1,000
Taxes & Licenses	1,000	500	500	500	500	500	500	500	500	500	500	500	500
Interest - Loan		563	558	553	547	542	537	532	527	522	517	512	507
Interest - Mortgage		1,333	1,331	1,329	1,328	1,326	1,324	1,322	1,320	1,318	1,316	1,315	1,313
Salaries		11,700	11,700	11,700	11,700	11,700	11,700	11,700	11,700	11,700	11,700	11,700	11,700
Advertising	1,000	1,000	750	500	500	500	750	500	500	500	750	500	500
Dues & Subscriptions		100											
Legal & Accounting	1,000	500	50	50	50	50	50	50	50	50	50	50	50
Office Supplies	200	150	150	150	150	150	150	150	150	150	150	150	150
Telephone	50	50	50	50	50	50	50	50	50	50	50	50	50
Utilities		800	800	800	800	800	800	800	800	800	800	800	800
Miscellaneous		1,500	1,500	1,500	1,500	1,500	1,500	1,500	1,500	1,500	1,500	1,500	1,500
Bank Loan Principal Pymt		644	649	653	658	663	668	673	678	683	688	694	699
Mortgage Principal Pymt		210	212	214	216	217	219	221	223	225	227	228	230
Equipment Purchases	25,000												
Total Expenses	$ 54,750	$ 27,025	$ 28,070	$ 32,949	$ 30,049	$ 31,088	$ 40,398	$ 48,078	$ 45,968	$ 43,298	$ 44,608	$ 45,099	$ 50,619
Ending Cash	$ 234,417	$ 221,343	$ 210,913	$ 205,864	$ 197,415	$ 190,507	$ 192,409	$ 201,991	$ 209,963	$ 215,265	$ 220,877	$ 227,978	$ 240,599

Year 2 Cash Flow Projections for THE MOUNTAIN SANDWICH SHOP

	January	February	March	April	May	June	July	August	Sept	Oct	Nov	Dec
Beginning Cash	$ 240,599	$ 246,270	$ 251,682	$ 267,843	$ 271,694	$ 264,969	$ 276,020	$ 291,932	$ 304,373	$ 308,474	$ 312,975	$ 318,876
Sales	$ 63,240	$ 57,120	$ 78,120	$ 54,000	$ 55,800	$ 68,400	$ 78,120	$ 70,680	$ 54,000	$ 55,800	$ 57,600	$ 78,120
Bank Loan												
Bank Loan Mortgage												
Shareholder's Loan												
Total Receipts	$ 63,240	$ 57,120	$ 78,120	$ 54,000	$ 55,800	$ 68,400	$ 78,120	$ 70,680	$ 54,000	$ 55,800	$ 57,600	$ 78,120
Purchases	$ 31,620	$ 28,560	$ 39,060	$ 27,000	$ 27,900	$ 34,200	$ 39,060	$ 35,340	$ 27,000	$ 27,900	$ 28,800	$ 39,060
Insurance	$ 500			$ 250			$ 250			$ 250		
Rent	$ 1,100	$ 1,100	$ 1,100	$ 1,100	$ 1,100	$ 1,100	$ 1,100	$ 1,100	$ 1,100	$ 1,100	$ 1,100	$ 1,100
Taxes & Licenses	$ 500	$ 500	$ 500	$ 500	$ 500	$ 500	$ 500	$ 500	$ 500	$ 500	$ 500	$ 500
Interest - Loan	$ 502	$ 496	$ 491	$ 486	$ 480	$ 475	$ 469	$ 464	$ 458	$ 453	$ 447	$ 441
Interest - Mortgage	$ 1,311	$ 1,309	$ 1,307	$ 1,305	$ 13,030	$ 1,301	$ 1,299	$ 1,297	$ 1,295	$ 1,293	$ 1,291	$ 1,289
Salaries	$ 15,000	$ 15,000	$ 15,000	$ 15,000	$ 15,000	$ 15,000	$ 15,000	$ 15,000	$ 15,000	$ 15,000	$ 15,000	$ 15,000
Advertising	$ 500	$ 750	$ 500	$ 500	$ 500	$ 750	$ 500	$ 500	$ 500	$ 750	$ 500	$ 500
Dues & Subscriptions	$ 100	$ 50	$ 50	$ 50	$ 50	$ 50	$ 50	$ 50	$ 50	$ 50	$ 50	$ 50
Legal & Accounting	$ 500											
Office Supplies	$ 150	$ 150	$ 150	$ 150	$ 150	$ 150	$ 150	$ 150	$ 150	$ 150	$ 150	$ 150
Telephone	$ 50	$ 50	$ 50	$ 50	$ 50	$ 50	$ 50	$ 50	$ 50	$ 50	$ 50	$ 50
Utilities	$ 800	$ 800	$ 800	$ 800	$ 800	$ 800	$ 800	$ 800	$ 800	$ 800	$ 800	$ 800
Miscellaneous	$ 2,000	$ 2,000	$ 2,000	$ 2,000	$ 2,000	$ 2,000	$ 2,000	$ 2,000	$ 2,000	$ 2,000	$ 2,000	$ 2,000
Bank Loan Principal Pymt	$ 704	$ 709	$ 715	$ 720	$ 725	$ 731	$ 736	$ 742	$ 748	$ 753	$ 759	$ 764
Mortgage Principal Pymt	$ 232	$ 234	$ 236	$ 238	$ 240	$ 242	$ 244	$ 246	$ 248	$ 250	$ 252	$ 255
Equipment Purchases	$ 2,000											
Total Expenses	$ 57,569	$ 51,708	$ 61,959	$ 50,149	$ 62,525	$ 57,349	$ 62,208	$ 58,239	$ 49,899	$ 51,299	$ 51,699	$ 61,959
Ending Cash	$ 246,270	$ 251,682	$ 267,843	$ 271,694	$ 264,969	$ 276,020	$ 291,932	$ 304,373	$ 308,474	$ 312,975	$ 318,876	$ 335,037

Year 3 Cash Flow Projections for THE MOUNTAIN SANDWICH SHOP

	January	February	March	April	May	June	July	August	Sept	Oct	Nov	Dec
Beginning Cash	$ 335,037	$ 332,511	$ 338,753	$ 356,524	$ 358,265	$ 349,430	$ 358,371	$ 375,893	$ 389,944	$ 391,935	$ 394,326	$ 398,117
Sales	$ 69,750	$ 63,000	$ 85,560	$ 54,000	$ 55,800	$ 68,400	$ 85,560	$ 78,120	$ 54,000	$ 55,800	$ 57,600	$ 85,560
Bank Loan												
Bank Loan Mortgage												
Shareholder's Loan												
Total Receipts	$ 69,750	$ 63,000	$ 85,560	$ 54,000	$ 55,800	$ 68,400	$ 85,560	$ 78,120	$ 54,000	$ 55,800	$ 57,600	$ 85,560
Purchases	$ 34,875	$ 31,500	$ 42,780	$ 27,000	$ 27,900	$ 34,200	$ 42,780	$ 39,060	$ 27,000	$ 27,900	$ 28,800	$ 42,780
Insurance	$ 500			250			250			250		
Rent	$ 1,200	1,200	1,200	1,200	1,200	1,200	1,200	1,200	1,200	1,200	1,200	1,200
Taxes & Licenses	$ 500	500	500	500	500	500	500	500	500	500	500	500
Interest - Loan	$ 502	496	491	486	480	475	469	464	458	453	447	441
Interest - Mortgage	$ 1,311	1,309	1,307	1,305	13,030	1,301	1,299	1,297	1,295	1,293	1,291	1,289
Salaries	$ 17,000	17,000	17,000	17,000	17,000	17,000	17,000	17,000	17,000	17,000	17,000	17,000
Advertising	$ 500	750	500	500	500	750	500	500	500	750	500	500
Dues & Subscriptions	$ 200											
Legal & Accounting	$ 500	50	50	50	50	50	50	50	50	50	50	50
Office Supplies	$ 150	150	150	150	150	150	150	150	150	150	150	150
Telephone	$ 60	60	60	60	60	60	60	60	60	60	60	60
Utilities	$ 800	800	800	800	800	800	800	800	800	800	800	800
Miscellaneous	$ 2,000	2,000	2,000	2,000	2,000	2,000	2,000	2,000	2,000	2,000	2,000	2,000
Bank Loan Principal Pymt	$ 704	709	715	720	725	731	736	742	748	753	759	764
Mortgage Principal Pymt	$ 232	234	236	238	240	242	244	246	248	250	252	255
Equipment Purchases	$ 11,242											
Total Expenses	$ 72,276	$ 56,758	$ 67,789	$ 52,259	$ 64,635	$ 59,459	$ 68,038	$ 64,069	$ 52,009	$ 53,409	$ 53,809	$ 67,789
Ending Cash	$ 332,511	$ 338,753	$ 356,524	$ 358,265	$ 349,430	$ 358,371	$ 375,893	$ 389,944	$ 391,935	$ 394,326	$ 398,117	$ 415,888